P.O. Box 1106

ISBN-13: 978-0-9859255-8-1
ISBN-10: 0-9859255-8-2

All artwork and photographs supplied by Anna Löwenadler.

First printing, December, 2013

Published by:

ThomasMax Publishing
P.O. Box 250054
Atlanta, GA 30325
www.thomasmax.com

P.O. Box 1106

by Anna Löwenadler

ThomasMax

Your Publisher
For The 21st Century

Introduction

P.O. Box 1106 is the true story of a very young girl who, along with her identical twin sister and seventeen-month-older brother, are forced to witness the attempted suicide of their mother. Those children also had a mentally disturbed father who was preoccupied with college and various jobs in an attempt to become a "nice Greek doctor," as his parents expected him to become. This story follows the hardships and brutal realities a girl and her siblings endured throughout their childhoods, while bringing to the forefront the damaging realities of dysfunctional families.

Overcoming adversities drives the human heart. Enduring a hopeless situation and expecting the result of nothing less is the surprising, unpredictable outcome of this story. Nothing is what it seems. In about 20,000 words, an unforeseen love story emerges between a Greek couple who can barely speak English and their three grandchildren during the mid-1970's. At a time when grandparents weren't expected to raise their grandchildren, this is a story about second chances. Realizing the disasters they created when raising their own son, changes and redirection are the only hopes they have to saving the spirits and the ultimate preservation of their grandchildren in this unhappy circumstance.

If you would like to contact me, please do so through ThomasMax Publishing.

-- Anna Löwenadler

To God,

for giving me my huband,

who has spent his life

mending my broken heart

Chapter 1

"The Day She Went Away"

I learned a very, very long time ago that wishing, wanting, hoping, and praying means absolutely nothing if the person you are doing it all for doesn't feel the same.

When I was three years old, going on four, I watched my mother frantically pace from the hallway bathroom to the kitchen. I heard her yelling and screaming profanities at my father as the green phone cord twisted into more and more tangled circles. I wondered how she was able to hold the phone at all since both her wrists had been cut again. I followed her around with my brother and sister and waited for the police to come because any time my mother was home, even briefly, the police usually came shortly after.

His name was Joey. I couldn't forget it even if I tried because we had friends that lived around the corner with whose brother, also named Joey, we often played. Thinking back, the police officer was probably very young but when you're little, everyone has a way of seeming much older than they actually are. I had never seen this particular officer before. He must have been new. All the others ones that had previously come knew our names, and so it was different having to go through the routine with a new policeman. He was extremely nice and friendly. He focused more on the three of us instead of my mother like all the officers had done before. He wouldn't take his eyes off of me, and his staring made me slightly uncomfortable.

I wasn't aware of all the blood. I had forgotten blood had such a profound smell, although in very small amounts it probably doesn't register. But on that day, in that bathroom, down our small hallway and into our even smaller kitchen, the large amount of blood smelled really, really bad.

By the time we settled outside in front of our house in a neighborhood selected for families with very low incomes, another police car had arrived and immediately joined the other -- strangely staring at us for what seemed like forever. And so for a while, we just all stood and stared at each other. I think they were in shock. Having experienced my mother's antics so many times before, I was used to it. I decided to stand around and wait for my father to come. When he arrived, within minutes the three men hoisted my mother into the back of the nearest police car. She continued her screaming and wailing as she had in the kitchen on the phone with my father. Now, however, she was holding a beer can.

None of us moved. Why would we? We had played this scene out with my mother so many times before. Maybe it was the penetrating Georgia heat or all the neighbors gathered outside our house shaking their heads again. Perhaps it was the drying of the blood all over our arms and faces. Whatever the reason, on that day, at that time, in that very moment, the decision my mother made to cut her wrists became the last time I ever hoped she would never do it again.

Rarely having your mother around changes everything. While my father was in college during the day and working various jobs at night, my mother spent her time riding around town on her green bicycle, meeting up with shady characters she called friends. She and her group spent their time together drinking and doing drugs. I had always thought my father knew, but as I became older, I realized that my father basically had no idea how we lived, where my mother went, or that my brother, sister, and I spent so much time by ourselves.

The day time was not so bad. We played outside. If we were lucky, my mother would have her "friends" over, and I felt a lot safer even if it meant carrying them beer all afternoon disguised in coke cans. My mother thought I was too dumb to smell the difference. Sometimes we would get hungry, but our mother had a habit of locking us out of the house. No matter how frustrating, we knew the routine, so my brother often climbed to look into my parents' window to keep us posted on what was happening. The day he saw my mother intimate with another man, the checking ended. After that, he never peeked again and we learned to ignore our hunger pains and use the bathroom outside.

Nights were dreadfully the hardest. Inside our house with just my brother and sister, I was so scared. I don't know how my brother managed to keep us calm but what he did for us when my mother was away was incredible. He gave us baths. He would go into the kitchen while my sister and I waited on the living room couch for him; he would bring us ketchup sandwiches he had made. He was really good at making them and this is what we ate every time we were left in his care. When we were done, he would hold my sister and me while he sat between us looking through the sheer living-room curtains, waiting for my mother to come home. She never would, and after so many hours, my brother would walk across the street and ask the lady who lived there to come and stay with us until my father could be called at work to come home.

My brother was only seventeen months older than my sister and me. My sister was only six minutes older than me. Every memory I ever had while we lived on South Tyler Court was that of my brother caring for my identical twin sister and me. I will never know how he felt, being placed in the role of both mother and father. I will never understand why he never seemed scared or how he became full just by watching my sister and I eat. One thing I did know: I knew I would never forgive my mother for putting my brother in that situation, and I will certainly never forgive my father for continuously allowing it to happen.

That day my mother was taken would be the last time in a long time we would see her. That same night, my father made us spend hours cleaning dried blood from the wall of our bathtub. We washed the ceiling and the rest of the bathroom only to continue with the floors and down the hall, into the kitchen where only more blood awaited.

I learned something very interesting about blood that night. When its red color dries, it becomes very black. No matter how hard you scrub your finger nails or how hard you wipe your hands, no matter how many times your wash your hair or hold your breath, the smell remains permanent and definite.

Chapter 2

"The Period Following"

My father made a lot of bad choices in his life. The first was marrying my American mother and the second was not becoming a nice Greek doctor. With my mother now institutionalized and he barely getting through college, my grandparents sold their store and farm and everything they had except their house to move in and help us.

I don't remember much about the initial arrangements, but the one thing I came to understand almost immediately is that my GaiGai (grandmother) did not like me, not even a little bit. During the years my grandparents lived with us, my grandmother called me "one spy." She spoke very broken English, with many of her words misused or mispronounced. Most of them were self-created but no matter her difficulties, I had no problem understanding what she meant. Referring to me as a spy was not a compliment.

My mother was institutionalized in a well-known mental facility in Milledgeville, Georgia, Central State Hospital. She was awarded structured and limited visitation with us after my parents divorced. Occasionally, while she was institutionalized, my father took my brother, my sister and me to visit her. She I did not like the way she looked. She always seemed incoherent and deranged. I could not understand how shocking someone made them better when, as far as I could tell, it looked an awful like killing instead. But shock treatment was standard fare in the early 1970's.

I later learned that the entire divorce took place while my mother was stuck in the facility with lots of other people who talked to themselves. She was diagnosed as bipolar with schizophrenic tendencies. Whatever her behaviors deemed, I always looked forward to seeing her and hoped that when I would, she might be allowed to stay.

My grandmother resented that I loved my mother. She despised my awaiting her visits. She hated my excitement and anticipation that the very next car that came up our street would be my mother's. GaiGai's posture stiffened and her lips tightened every time my mother actually showed. She was always ready to tell us that she knew she wouldn't come.

On one such visit, my mother and grandmother got into a very heated argument. My mother, filled with so much rage, slapped my grandmother's glasses completely off her face. The glasses flew across the kitchen until they rested atop the stove. Holding firm to the wall right beside, my grandmother looked and saw me standing, watching the whole fight when she thought I was in my room as she had instructed. I had earned the name spy. I turned and ran down the hallway and jumped into my bed. Shortly thereafter, my mother left without being allowed to say good-bye. She never came back, and that was the last time we saw her on South Tyler Court.

Hearing my grandmother use certain words made it easy to know who she was calling for or talking about. My father, on the other hand, made his name calling for us extremely difficult because he never consistently referred to us by the same name. For the longest time, I thought my name was, "Jesus fucking Christ." I always went to him when I heard that name until one time he said he was expecting my brother. Through the confusion, the three of us realized that his name calling depended on the day. My father was intensely explosive. Every single memory I ever had of my father involved some kind of demonic behavior. With absolute certainty, my father hated my brother, sister and me but he particularly found my brother repulsive.

As hard as it is to admit, my father enjoyed torturing my brother. He made no excuses for punching my brother anywhere, anytime. My father had no problem hurting any of the three of us, but his beatings seemed so much more intense and vulgar when they were afflicted on my brother. GaiGai often intervened and tried to keep my father away from my brother, but somehow he managed to find a way to beat my brother daily. The only time my father stopped hurting my brother was the brief seconds he took catching his breath so he could continue a little longer.

All of our interactions with our father were generally unpleasant. As far back as I can remember, just my father's presence gave me severe stomach pains. I couldn't handle watching my father mistreat the only person who had given me so much love. I hated myself. I still hate myself. Everything my father did to my brother was so wrong and vile, and yet there was absolutely nothing I could do about it.

As my brother, sister and I grew, my temper got meaner and at various times I found myself "falling" in the way of my brother or sister long enough to take the blows intended for them. My father beat us all the time. When he wasn't beating us, he was calling for one of us to beat. The outcome was always the same. I cried. He beat more while yelling in my ears about the pointlessness of crying. Hearing his words just made me weep more.

Our very small three-bedroom house became increasingly smaller when my grandparents moved in. My father slept across the hall from my sister and me. Up the hallway my grandfather (Pau Pou) and my brother slept in the third bedroom, which put my grandmother on a pull-out couch that permanently stayed in our living room.

GaiGai took on the role of mother, and in so many ways made our lives better, although it was still unbearable. For all the hate my father had for my brother, my grandmother had just the opposite. She absolutely adored him. Not only did she favor him, she did everything for him so that my father wouldn't get as mad. Before my grandmother came, my brother had to do all the chores my mother neglected. GaiGai made it her mission to take them over. I thought she did a great job, a lot better than my brother ever could.

My grandmother loved and cared for my sister just as well but when it came to me . . . well, my grandmother did not like me at all. She often compared me to my mother and said that I was just like her. So since she hated my mother, hating me came naturally.

During the years the five of us all lived together, my father periodically and oddly would nicely asked us if we wanted to play with him. As confused as we were, we liked playing games. "Hide and seek" in the house was a particular favorite of mine, because it involved my father picking me up and hiding me in our hallway closet. There was no way the seeker would ever know to look up and find me sitting Indian style, on the top shelf.

When my father went to bathe us, he often got into the tub and I loved playing "Barber Shop." Combing the hair on his head and other parts of his body was all part of playing. I was too young to realize his inappropriate nature. Looking back, I'm sickened by how much I thought holding his penis with two hands was fun. Waving it around and talking to it like I did with my "Hollie Hobbie" dolls until white stuff came out all over me made my father smile with his eyes closed. I thought he really liked this game because he wanted to play it a lot.

This life we lived continued and between the beatings and abuse, my father initiated a new game, one we had never played before. The game was actually very simple and one we all wanted to win. My father would take a broom stick straw from our kitchen's broom and break it into three pieces. Holding them perfectly aligned in front of us, the one who picked the shortest piece got to sleep with him that night. Since none of us had ever slept with him, not even when my mother lived with us, we thought it would be fun. The best part was getting to wear one of my father's white t -shirts because on us, it was so long. When either my sister or I got to wear it, we pretended to be a bride walking down the aisle.

I will never forget the first time I had won the coveting game. I had no idea what my brother or sister were expecting when they won, but I couldn't wait to leap on the side of the bed where my mother had always slept. I had hopes that maybe; just maybe, I might be able to smell her smell once more. I wondered if there was a chance that I would be able to find stains of her red lipstick still dyed on the pillow she once laid her head. I couldn't wait to see if I would be lucky enough to find a piece of her brown hair still clinging to the bed sheets or better, a ball of it down in the railings. I didn't tell my brother or sister what I was wishing. I didn't want them to get to any of my mother before me. I didn't want them to ruin my anticipation. I didn't want them spoil my surprise.

No one needed to tell me that what my father did to me that night or what my father made me do to him that same night was wrong. I just knew. Everything that I dreamed about sleeping in the biggest bed in the house became one occurring nightmare after another until my father was finished playing.

My heart hurt so much that without even thinking, I had to hold both my hands firmly against my chest. The crying sounds the thumping made were so loud, I was afraid that my father would hear them and become angry. I stayed there, paralyzed, quiet and still until I thought my father had fallen asleep and then hurried across the hallway into my bed.

Whoever I was before I picked the shortest broomstick straw or who I thought I was before I slept with my father that night, was not the same person I awoke to the following morning. The whore my grandmother said that I would become like my mother had come so much sooner than I had imagined. Now, at the age of four, the name fit me perfectly and I could no longer feel bad when she addressed me as such.

As time passed in much the same way, my sister randomly approached me about the "broomstick" game. She wanted to know if my father and I played the version like she was forced to with him and when I confessed, she privately went to GaiGai and told.

Although my brother was a participant in the "broomstick" game, he never discussed those events with my sister and me. I therefore assumed this abuse was reserved for us twin girls only. My brother got enough physical abuse from my father. Years later he confirmed to me that he was not sexually molested.

Once GaiGai found out about the situation, we moved three hours away into our grandparents' farm house the summer before I started second grade.

Chapter 3

"The Move"

I imagined the house had been beautiful at one time. It was an incredibly large colonial set in the country where the nearest neighbor resided about two miles down the road. Enormous Doric columns lining the front porch now stood cracked with white paint shillings dusting the weathered wooden floor. Woven rockers awaiting visitors to sit and wave off annoying gnats in the suffocating Georgia heat no longer adorned the porch.

Two large doors I never once saw open led directly into a conservative foyer with a nine-foot vaulted ceiling. Instead of the traditionally seen ravishing wall paintings and furnishings, this entry was nothing more than storage to an old noisy freezer rarely seen by those other than our family.

The house itself had an open floor plan with wonderfully large rooms designed for entertaining. And although the light fixtures were a bit extravagant with the capacity of holding at least six light bulbs, there were never more than one bulb in any of them. Aside of a few family photographs, countless water stains decorated the walls and wallpaper while oriental rugs blanketing the hardwood floors had all been eaten on by pesky mice in search of food. The simple furniture arranged throughout the living room bore numerous yellow stains of children who for some reason had failed with every attempt to reach at least one of the two bathrooms on the first floor of the house. Instead of elaborate fireplaces, every room was warmed by propane gas heaters that were just as scary to ignite as they were to turn off. The kitchen, however plain, happened to be my favorite room of all because no matter the time of day, amazing aromas could be smelled throughout. Upstairs was another house entirely. My grandparents periodically rented it out to subsidize their income. As long as we lived there, with the exception of one family, it stayed dormant.

Outside, the house was surrounded by acres of land with dozens of fruit and nut trees. Across the dirt road and on both sides of my grandparents' house were fields of corn, peanuts and tobacco. Behind the house stood a rundown barn that when I was very young, held the most beautiful horses I had ever seen, including my very own. Now only stacks of black screen doors laid against the back wall where once more than thirty rattlers had been found and men from town came to help kill them all. The local paper took pictures and wrote a story all about it. I'm not sure how no one got bit, I'm just glad we weren't living there at the time.

All that was left now was a very tired woman in a very old house with an even older husband and three young grandchildren that were anything but innocent.

My grandmother was worn. Her hands and arms looked a lot like leather and even though I still saw her as beautiful with an olive glow, her face was extremely wrinkled. Her eyes always seemed so sad. I often wondered what they would say had they not been so silenced by the tears she wept when she didn't think anyone was looking. She had worked awfully hard for a very long time with my grandfather uptown in their restaurant and store, starting her day at four in the morning and ending well after ten that evening.

Instead of a life of serenity and peace in the house she spent years paying for but not really being allowed to enjoy, she had a new job, a new work day. Another hardship and added pain had been placed on her by another, for another, in the hopes of saving her three small others.

Every day, my grandmother fought hard to maintain her sanity. We had repressed so much turmoil and horror so deep within that without warning, we suddenly exploded to this renaissance and acceptance of a woman who hadn't the slightest idea to what she had just opened her home .

Without the luxury of television or radio, we often entertained ourselves by torturing our beloved grandmother. At least once a week, the only separation between GaiGai and one of us was the dining room table. Seeing her blue-tinted hair, which she swore was a natural rinse, flying about and her hands shaking in distress calling out the help of Saint Mary and Jesus in Greek, was absolute hysterical sight. We knew that once through the dining room doors, age would prevail and eventually GaiGai would give up after countless circles around and around. So with a quick swig of her "medicine"(ouzo) she kept in the china cabinet, the battle would end with meaningless threats of spankings she would give before we went to sleep at night.

Before long, the five of us found ourselves living day to day just like we thought other families lived. Since GaiGai could barely speak proper English, it was no surprise that the three of us periodically took turns filling out checks to which our grandmother only signed her name. Once they were properly addressed, my sister and I were expected take and retrieve mail from the post office about seven miles away.

With a packed lunch and detailed lecture, forbidding us to walk the railroad tracks as a short cut and an added reminder of our post office box number 1106, we were handed walking sticks that looked more like backscratchers, intended to protect us from runaway dogs. As always, we promised GaiGai that we would not walk the tracks and just as always, we most certainly did.

On one of those trips it began to rain. The rain came fast, and my sister and I were caught off guard. Those droplets hit us hard in the face, soaking us within seconds as we gave the word sprint a whole new meaning. Just outside the post office and directly on the disallowed tracks, we ran on those slippery metal snakes as hard as our legs could carry us. I ignored the vibrations underneath my feet. I knew what was coming but chose to convince myself it was just my shivering until, without warning, the whistle blew and that train came upon us, faster than even the rain fell. There was just time enough to see my sister jump to the opposite side of me, screaming and clinging to a miniature bridge which overlooked an underpass. I felt certain she had fallen over. Like any raging train, the wind was furious and loud, so loud my cries could have never been heard as projectile vomit winded to the next town. Within minutes, everything around me stood silent and still. I wasn't exactly sure what to do. I didn't want to look over and not see my sister but I had to know where she was, so with my hands covering my squinted eyes, I peeked through my fingers and for the very first time in my life, being an identical twin had meaning. Looking over at her, I was looking at me.

My tears of agony were her tears of joy when she turned and saw me standing there, her faced pressed against the cold concrete, as I called out her name, choking on my soaking wet hair. That day bonded us in an unexplainable way. No matter how different we would remain from each other, no matter her preference for my brother instead of me, no matter how hard GaiGai pegged her against me, no matter what, she and I would always be one, as long as we had each other. Waiting out the storm under a giant pecan tree, we gathered ourselves together and started back home.

Entering the house, GaiGai sat us at the table with warm, cooked buttermilk she must have been making while we were gone. She didn't ask a single question or say one word about the lack of mail. She just stared at our swollen red eyes as we sat there sipping our milk, thanked the Mother Mary for our return in Greek and walked away.

Getting through a week was long, much longer for my grandmother, so Sunday came as a blessing. The night before, was slept in paper napkin rollers

twisted up in our hair so that my sister and I could be
glared at, cross-eyed, by every purple-haired lady in
the pews around us. My brother was the lucky one. All
he had to do was make sure he kept his shirt tucked in
his pants as he escorted Gai Gai to her invisible
reserved seat, established from the first day she became
a "member" there.

Being at church was nothing compared to getting
to there without anyone seeing us in Gai Gai's antique
white Chevrolet. My siblings and I had all mastered the
skill of lying face down on the floor boards of that old
car without messing up our clothes or hair. Our
grandmother was a horrible driver. One of us had to sit
in the long front seat and assist her driving inabilities.
That poor unfortunate soul was usually me. No matter
how hard I tried, I could never explain to GaiGai that
cars indeed had the tendency to blind her when she
made it a habit of driving in their lanes. She never
grasped this concept. None of the screaming and
hollering she did ever made the cars move away; if
anything, they just got closer. I cannot believe that we
never got into an accident or damaged the car by
veering constantly on and off the road.

Getting past the parked cars in the church
parking lot was so much easier than parallel parking
such a long car without the comfort of power steering. I
am convinced that this act alone is what made GaiGai
so disproportioned. Her arms were enormous and giant
compared to the rest of her body. I found it hard not to
look at her muscles growing in size every time she

pulled on the steering wheel, backing up and pulling forward until finally coming to a stop.

She did not share in our embarrassment. GaiGai was not the least bit ashamed of her car. She drove that tank like a Cadillac with the papers still attached to its window, all the while reminding us how fortunate we were to at least have a car. She had no problem waving her hands at us, yelling that although old, her car was paid off and therefore better than riding in a brand new one, which would be technically owned by the bank. Whatever her point, the subject was always dismissed as soon as the car came to rest and my brother, sister and I jumped out, blending in with the parking lot congestion before we thought anyone would recognize us.

Chapter 4

"Work Work and More Work"

The end of the week meant only the beginning of a new one, and life at GaiGai's was one of long working days that seem to never end. Almost everything we ate was homemade. Pasta (orzo) took hours. A bowl full of dough separated and methodically rolled into teeny tiny nuggets that looked just like rice was intended to be eaten on a later date. Countless hours were spent popping, peeling, cutting, washing, drying, storing, and canning every fruit and vegetable we grew on that farm. My God, I hated every minute of it! Even "off" days, were hard. On any given day, upon returning home from school we were instructed to walk ever so softly, staying clear of our beds because bread was rising in them all. I didn't care. When my brother and sister were preoccupied with each other, I used to sneak down the hallway to my room and go right up to my bed. I would yank the bed spread up as high as I could and then jump one really hard time on the floor in protest for what I considered a stupid routine. Rows of bread were sitting on shelves at the "Piggly Wiggly" GaiGai went to every week, so I found no reason why she couldn't just buy it there. Hard work was all it seemed GaiGai knew, and we were taught almost immediately that being poor was the ultimate incentive to work even harder. We learned that lesson every single day.

I dreaded laundry day. Not my brother of course, as laundry was women's work. Though washing clothes was not bad, carrying out the heavy loads with my sister, without capsizing in 95 freaking degrees was nearly impossible. Everything about hanging laundry was systematic. GaiGai had a particular and precise way of how she expected clothes to be hung. My sister and I were well aware of her methods and so it was no surprise that hanging clothes became an all-day affair. Not once, not one time did we ever get away with hanging clothes on the first try. As long as we lived at GaiGai's, my sister and I were made to hang again what had just been hung until GaiGai approved. Sometimes, I think her repetitive nature was nothing more than a ploy to keep us out of her hair. Driving the pole up into the air while steadying and securing the bottom half into the ground could only be defined successful when neither of us suffered any external injuries and we both walked away with our eyes still intact.

Standing there watching our garments sway in the hot wind was a beautiful sight. Looking at the sleeves dance about, harmonizing their patterns all by the strength of a single clothes pin was symbolically profound. If one of the pins came undone, the line of togetherness would be broken and no longer visually, as lovely.

GaiGai had the knack of teaching us lessons without saying anything at all. She didn't have to. The calluses on all of our hands and the bigger ones on our feet, the sweat permanently dripping off our faces and the secrets we would keep, were all the words needed.

On days that PauPou was well enough to venture out, my siblings and I prepared ourselves for a back-breaking day of the hardest, most intense labor that even a crew of grown men would have had trouble enduring.

My brother's favorite color was red. Because of this declaration, he always got to use the red sling. My sister and I were left to fight over the remaining two. One resembled the letter L and was the heaviest. The other looked like my brother's, in the shape of a half moon, and was just as light. Of course I got stuck with the heaviest. I always did. I didn't want GaiGai to hear my sister crying and then start wheezing with asthma. I had experienced the outcome of that before. My grandmother came running out the kitchen door, cussing me in Greek and "fixing me" good with a stick. I got tired of that happening, so I learned to drag that heavy sling behind me and pray that when we got to slinging, I wouldn't cut my legs as deep or reopen scars from the time before.

Slinging was brutal, but pulling honeysuckle vines from a fence we never saw was downright mortifying. Bumblebees absolutely love honeysuckle. We could not convince my grandfather of this simple observation. He instead constantly drove our hands and faces deeper into the vines while blood collected around our wrists, as gloves were generally thought worthless because of their size. For some reason, the bees really liked me. Without sharing mutual regard, I spent most of my time slapping my arms about like a plane propeller. This merely intensified their family and friends to court me with hundreds of stings about my ears and head.

Only when I was no longer recognizable and PauPou had made additional welts on my back with his handy walking stick called a *bastuni*, blaming me for my misfortune, was I allowed refuge in the house where GaiGai granted herself permission to whip me more. I guess it was better that I couldn't see her coming. Besides, I was in so much pain, her blows didn't even matter.

Although just as back-breaking, weeding the peanut fields at least gave us freedom from our grandfather. All we had to do was walk up and down the aisles of peanuts and remove any plant threatening the growth of the potential profit. If ever a peanut plant had accidentally been pulled, we would quickly and quietly replant it knowing all-to-well the repercussions of our actions. Most of the time, my sister and I took turns jumping over the rows singing and dancing, waiting for GaiGai to call us in for supper.

On a particularly hot day, my sister had chosen to dance her way closer to a line of trees, next to the edge of dirt road we never gone down, so we had no idea where it led. I was distracted from her in the shade by an unusual, strange high-pitched sound I had never heard before. I knew my sister did not know how to whistle but the sound seemed to be coming right out of her. Before I had the chance to open my mouth, a man peered thru the trees! Not a regular man, a naked one. A man that knew how to whistle and one that was trying to get the attention of my sister and me by using his hand on his penis the way my father did when I had to sleep with him.

Everything became a blur. I started screaming! I started running. I went for my sister and told her to head straight towards me so we could get across the street into our yard. I told her not to turn around. I didn't want her to see to what she had been so close. We got across. We made it all the way inside, directly into the kitchen where PauPou was sitting at his usual spot by the window and GaiGai by hers, at the stove. They weren't ready for us. I starting slamming shut every opened window I saw and locking every opened door until I got to the back bedroom where I saw my brother's .22-gauge shotgun leaning against his closet. I grabbed it, ran back to the kitchen where my sister was telling our grandparents what I had seen. GaiGai took the gun and headed up our driveway, across the dirt road in search of the man not wearing any clothes. No sooner did she cross when a fully dressed man wearing blue jeans roared around her, kicking up red dust on a motorcycle my sister and I never heard. We never saw him or had to weed that peanut field again.

Other days were spent picking fruit from the various trees PauPou still watered and fed so we could help GaiGai later can them for winter. While my brother picked bruised ones already lying on the ground, my sister and I had the frightening duty of climbing and picking them from the high branches because we knew that if she only got the bruised ones, we would be sent out again to get more.

There was one tree of which my sister and I were very afraid. We were terrified of the fig tree. We always saved that tree for last. Snakes love figs, so my sister and I took turns watching out for them. One of us had to constantly turn and walk around the tree, eyeing up every limb, making sure to forewarn the one climbing if a snake was sighted. There is nothing more paralyzing than pulling what feels like a fig, then quickly realizing it is the head of a snake instead. I wish I could admit that this only occasionally happened, but it seemed to occur almost every time I was the one climbing. Avoiding fig stains while trying to fill an entire basket was another job in itself. I didn't care that GaiGai used my sister as the perfect example of a diligent worker who could finish with a white apron. Limiting burgundy stains was the least of my concerns. Snake patrol should have been the real focus. I made it mine, anyway.

Every Friday before my father came to visit, my grandmother sent my siblings and me around the yard to collect fallen tree branches -- and then into the front where tons of chestnut balls awaited in multitudes. For me, picking up miniature porcupines was the absolute worst job because it was impossible to get them without completely cutting up our bare feet. Our shoes were saved for going to town. Calluses built up over time were no match for the penetrating needles, no matter how selectively I tiptoed. Learning the skill of simultaneously holding two sticks together without dropping the ball before landing it in the opened paper sack GaiGai gave us was purely luck. But cleaning the yard and putting everything in order was an act my grandmother thought would soften the tension of my father's visit.

Chapter 5

"The Visits"

My father came to visit almost every weekend. I never really understood why he even bothered since none of us, including my grandparents, looked forward to seeing him. Still he came and I dreaded his stay. I viewed them as a simple reminder of a life I never wanted. Other children were born and given a life, I had been born and given a purpose --his.

My mother's choice of using drugs and alcohol was far more desirable than being burdened with the responsibility of three small children. Her lack of presence left a permanent hole in my heart that no amount of tears, no matter how many, would ever be able to fill. Clumps of violent frustration seemed to multiply every time I saw my father's face as it reminded me of her very existence.

We never talked about my mother. I guess in life, some things are just better left unsaid or in our case, kept a secret. GaiGai branded in our minds that what happens in the family stays in the family. To honor your family meant to protect it.

As soon as he came, my brother, sister and I reluctantly approached him, knowing that within minutes his demeanor would change into that of horrific rage with yelling and cursing soon to follow. My father was extremely peculiar with OCD tendencies, and I think in some ways, we were reminders of failure. The fact that he had his parents doing his rendering only intensified an already volatile situation.

My grandmother tried so hard. She carefully took time to fix our hair, braiding and pulling it back away from our faces, while my brother had his done in the barber chair. None of those efforts mattered. My father always found something inappropriate with what we were wearing and never had anything positive to say.

One visit in particular I wish I could forget. My sister and I were wearing red nail polish. I thought I looked wonderful. I felt just like Barbie. I couldn't wait for my father to see how pretty my nails were. I was wrong. Whether it was the color or just the fact we were wearing it, something about it drove my father over the edge.

Instead of using nail polish remover or allowing us to remove it ourselves, he took a pocket knife and chiseled every single nail. I almost lost consciousness when the color began to mix with my bleeding fingers. All the commotion confused my father, making him even angrier.

To this very day, although faint, ridges can still be seen on many of my nails. I never wear red nail polish. I won't even hold a bottle of it. The memory of that day is just too permanent.

Asking to see our schoolwork was another travesty. He was very aware that my sister and I struggled with our subjects, especially math. For hours, my sister and I were forced to sit at the kitchen table doing multiplication and division, holding pencils from which he had ripped the erasers "because his children didn't make mistakes."

In reluctant desperation, I would lick my finger and gently wipe the paper, accidentally rubbing a hole in place of my incorrect answers. I could sense the excitement on my father's face. This was exactly what he was waiting for, justification for the repeated punching of my head until my sister made her own mistakes, and the closed hands would be divided between us. Like clockwork, his temperament would change and for reasons I'll never fully understand. His hostility would become softer and the yelling would become quieter, and a more tolerant father would emerge.

My father usually had a planned agenda for the four of us when he came on the weekends. If it was hot . . . and it usually was during the summer . . . he would take us swimming at the only public pool in town. There we would swim well into the evening. The pool was always packed with people. So much congestion was intimidating to me, as was the fear of swimming. I didn't know how to properly swim. In those days, doggie paddling was an acceptable form for most. Kicking your feet while holding your breath under water for long periods of time is what my brother did, so I considered him, an advanced swimmer.

At the pool, giant, massive inner tubes were not only permanently stationed, but permitted in the water. Big kids would stack them on top of each other, creating enormous pyramids that could be seen about the pool. My brother was allowed to go off alone, but my sister and I had to swim with our father close by.

Had I known that bobbing down would mean a matter a life and death, never would I have ventured into the water at all. Seconds felt like minutes. Trapped underneath a stack of tubes, breathing in water instead of air, I momentarily blacked out.

When I finally came around and tried to make sense of what had just happened, I couldn't believe that my father had actually saved me from drowning. By yanking on both of my feet and pulling me up out of the water, I survived. I decided then that even though my father had one body, he was really two different people: one was a person that could have love, compassion, gentleness, etc., and a second person that had none. My brush with death that day was the only time I ever came in contact with the nice person living inside my father's body.

Going swimming was the only part of my father's visits I enjoyed. Aside from his wicked temper, he was a perfectionist and thus demanded absolute perfection from his children. As brutal as he was in his expectations, they seemed to intensify around my brother. There is no other way to explain that from almost the very beginning of my brother's life, it seemed to me that my father despised him. I believe that my father hated my brother more than GaiGai could ever hate me. Even though we were all subjected to his verbal humiliations, his psychotic rampages most often were directed solely towards my brother. As much as I hated watching my brother suffer, I hated myself more for silently being relieved that for a moment my brother was enduring the wrath of my father instead of me.

I have never seen another human being pleasure himself from the cruelty invoked on another than that of my father towards my brother. It is hard to understand how he could still feel worthy to call him his son. The reasons my father hurt my brother so much must have been the same ones GaiGai had every time she sent me down the hall to sleep with my father when he visited, knowing exactly what would happen when she did.

Like all the times before, I floated outside of my body. I watched myself lying there, helpless and hopeless until I couldn't take what I was seeing any longer. In order to save me, I had to abandon me. I pleaded to myself to believe that once or twice a week was far better than all the times prior when living with my father on South Tyler Court.

I never waved as hard as I did, then when it came time for my father to leave. The next visit would come too soon and be all too familiar, a seemingly never-ending conclusion to an ongoing nightmare.

Chapter 6

"Stuck Indoors"

As the summer months ended and the last of the leaves fell, winter brought the five of us closer than we wanted to be. All the rooms except our bedrooms were closed off to conserve heat, so most of our time was spent in the kitchen.

Occasionally, GaiGai would call out to us that she needed meat from the "freezer room." Any time we heard those dreadful words, we silently hoped and prayed we weren't anywhere near her. This was a very unwanted and unenvied task. We never answered. We knew better. But eventually through the rules of rotation, an unlucky soul had no choice but to journey into the cold and darkness.

There were only two rooms to pass through. As simple as it seems, it was just the opposite. The dining room went directly into the living room, which led to the infamous door that opened to the "freezer room." Both rooms were pitch black and freezing cold. Being in them alone was mortifying. Every step intensified the fear that "something" was going to get you. While the two lucky ones stayed behind with their ears pressed tightly to the door waiting the call of help, the other one ran at record speed with eyes closed, straight towards the door harboring the dreadful, antique keyhole.

This was the deciphering moment of life or death! If the door failed to cooperate and the skull key wouldn't fit, the one whose turn it was would struggle every second, waiting to fall prey to whatever was lurking inside. Just when the shaking hands and panic became uncontrollable, the door would click open as it always did, and cheers could be heard from the awaiting two.

Unfortunately, getting the door open was nothing compared to finding the only light. The switch just happened to be a five-foot dirty white string that seemed to grow shorter with every crucial second. Waving your hands back and forth spastically in the air, hoping that no one else would grab it before you did, was too much.

The string we worried we'd never find would finally be in hand and yanked with supernatural powers in the foyer with the noisy freezer that held the precious meat. Locating the right package without having to pry it from anything else frozen to it was a God-given miracle.

As time seemed to stop, so did the other two, waiting for the sound of pounding feet that bounded back through the darkened rooms to the kitchen door. A pale-faced child stormed with meat clinched securely against his or her face.

After dinner, bedtime was usually around nine o'clock in the evening. Dressed in flannel hand-sewn nightgowns and beneath layers of heater blankets, GaiGai often lay with my sister and me, telling various stories of her own childhood while my brother in the next room listened in.

When her stories were over and the three of us almost asleep, GaiGai would make her way out of our frigid room, down the hall to the bedroom where she and PauPou slept in separate twin beds.

One night when she had barely reached her door frame, GaiGai heard my sister and me screaming at the top of our lungs that we were on fire. Running back into our room, she watched as my sister and I popped and sparked like hundreds of firecrackers. Static electricity was not a term with which we were familiar. Believing that we would catch on fire by even the slightest movement (without actually being on fire) meant the exact same thing to my sister and me. After much consoling and convincing, joined by our brother, those gowns were immediately removed, and we never wore them again!

Staying warm during the cold winter nights was not nearly as difficult as making ourselves think that the constant noises surrounding our rooms were not those of giant wolf rats. Before moving to GaiGai's, such an animal was unknown. We learned very quickly that GaiGai's house was different from other houses, and things that went on there just didn't go on anywhere else.

At first, the three of us were disappointed that we had never been privileged enough to come across one of these mysterious animals. We wondered what they looked like and if their appearance matched the name. Wolf rat? Oh, I don't think so. This small animal was more like a miniature possum. Sometimes gray, sometimes brown, the color didn't seem to matter.

Their whips, disguised as tails, were incredibly long with eyes almost as big as ours and teeth that hung past their bottom lips. When my brother, sister, and I took turns hitting the walls while we lay in bed at night, the wolf rats would screech like fighting alley cats, claiming territory that was already inhabited. We never got used to hearing the sounds that came from within our walls.

To keep them from entering, GaiGai came up with a fabulous idea. With collected tin can lids, the four of us took on the tedious task of nailing the freshly painted white tops to the baseboards of our rooms. Every time a giant new hole appeared, we would get another one and cover it. I didn't mind the painting part and even credit the wolf rats for my passion of art. The paint brushes we used were made from cut pine straw needles tied together by saved rubber bands. I thought GaiGai was a genius. When we got done using them, we simply threw them away. New ones could be made in a matter of seconds. Brilliant, purely brilliant.

With the leftover paint, I used to find intricate pieces of wood around the old barn to detail. Then I would pretend to be a salesman and sell them to GaiGai for a penny. My sister also profited but since she lacked my painting abilities, she made simple braided vine bracelets so she could play salesman too.

Chapter 7

"Games"

Finding ways to deal with boredom, my brother led the way by making up games using things we found around the house. Inventing various ways of having fun meant creating the rules as well. Since most of the ideas were my brother's, my sister and I basically did whatever he said because all we wanted to do was play. One of the first games I can ever remember my brother inventing was a game called, "ball in the hall."

There was only one hallway in our entire house. Separated by a bathroom on one end and a room we called the telephone room on the other, two of us sat, opposite each other, anxiously rolling a ball back and forth. The one left out was the referee. The objective should have been simple. If the ball bounced, or rolled so hard it went over the player's leg, the referee would call the ball out and thus a point was given to the other player.

My brother had a way of manipulating the ruling every time it wasn't in his favor. My sister and I got tired of him always complaining that the ball didn't actually go over the leg but that it merely "touched' the leg. If we dared not give him more points, he would start yelling and before long, GaiGai would get involved and next thing you know, she's in the china cabinet grabbing at her "medicine bottle".

"Pull off socks" was a game we stole from watching a children's show called, "Zoom." This game allowed all three of us to play together. Cheating was virtually impossible. The one remaining with at least one sock still on one of his or her feet while the others lost both of theirs would be the winner. I use to lose at this game a lot so, once I decided to put on a brand new pair of polyester long ones. I thought for sure, that this, without a doubt, would be the one way I would finally be named, the victor.

My strategy was better than I had hoped. My brother went at my socks with such force that before I had a chance to react, my toes folded on top of each other and crossed like a Chinese yoyo. The pain in my face only added to his excitement. Screaming that my choice of socks was a direct violation of the rules, he granted himself permission to teach me a lesson. Looking over at my sister, I could see that even she was at a loss for words. I guess she thought that if she mentioned how angry GaiGai would be if she found out that my brother was ruining the only good pair of socks I had, then maybe he would stop. He did not. Not until a tiny hole emerged between my big and second toes and I started crying, threatening to go tell GaiGai, did he quit.

Most of the time, GaiGai made us play outside so PauPou could rest in his bed. We used to follow my brother around, waiting for him to come up with something new we could do.

One day, in a matter of seconds, my brother said he had a great idea. Instead of throwing away an empty milk jug our grandmother had given him, he decided to fill it up with water. My sister and I didn't really understand his motive until he found a very large stick and proceeded to beat the living crap out of it, all over the yard. He named the game, "beat the milk jug." I thought it was a perfect name, although vile and disturbing. Unfortunately, the game often ended as soon as it started so my brother was the only one that got a turn to play it.

My siblings were very close. Even though my sister and I were the twins, she and my brother acted more like a pair, and neither of them liked me very much at all. Most of the time, I played alone or watch them play together. "Stuntman" was a game I was happy not to play but one that the two of them played all the time. I didn't even like watching them play it.

Outside our house when the home was rebuilt, a very high set of wooden stairs my brother oiled once a year allowed passage to the top floor without disturbing the family living below. A small platform separated the bottom stairs from the higher ones, and this is where the game of "Stuntman" took place.

My brother would wait with an invisible camera on the grass until my sister reached the platform. When he yelled, "Action," my sister would leap in random positions all the way to the ground. The more violent the stunt, the better the cheering and so my sister would continue trying more dangerously then before, over and over again.

Only idiots would find amusement in watching what looked like a tortured soul having an epileptic seizure or worse, a demonic possession. But that is exactly what I considered the two of them -- idiots.

When my brother thought my sister needed a break, they would move to the front yard where a massive chestnut tree grew. My brother would literally hang my sister with a rope that he tied between her legs and leave her hanging from a limb for hours, occasionally bringing her crackers and water. This game did not have a name. I called it stupid! She liked it though, and even when she had trouble sleeping at night because of the nasty bruises on her inner thighs, she played that game whenever he wanted.

In the evening when PauPou was feeling better, he made the three of us play cards. Black Jack and Twenty-One were his favorites. Twenty pennies were given to my brother, sister and me. This was our official betting money, and sign that the card playing would begin. My grandfather didn't care how late into the night we played. Even when we begged to go to bed or lose all of our money, he would spot us additional pennies and make us keep playing. He was always the dealer. If a card happened to fall, he quickly covered it with his "bastuni," telling us in Greek to keep our eyes on the table. He never lost, not a single time.

The most notorious and best game of all time could only be played at night, in the dark. Directly on the left side of our house was a corn field. When the corn had finally grown in and was almost at the peak of picking, we loved to play, "hide and seek" in the corn rows.

Since my brother was in charge of the games, he was the one who got to carry the only flashlight we had. During the daylight hours, the corn field didn't look scary at all, but at night, there was something terrifying about the sound corn husks make when the wind blows thru them. Nighttime insects added to the fear because their sounds multiplied as we ran past them, row to row.

On the count of three, my brother, sister, and I would dart as fast as we could until we disappeared from each other into the blackness. To find two perfect corn stalks where I could cramp down and wait to hear the others coming, made my heart pound. There will never be enough words to describe how it feels when, out of nowhere, someone grabs you by the hair and yanks your arm at the same time. I will admit there were times I peed my pants.

All the running made us hot and tired. While we knew this, we also knew the consequences of removing our jackets or long-sleeved shirts. If one of us was seen trying, the other two heeded the warnings but it never failed. In almost every game, one of us would over heat and remove the unthinkable.

Why was that unthinkable? Corn husks hurt. Running through rows of corn while the husks whip you all over can be detrimental. Taking off our only protection meant that tiny slashes would accumulate all over our faces, arms and hands. Sweating profusely added to the problem. The mistake of cooling off while your upper body burned diabolically is what finally ended the game.

Mercurochrome was the "cure all" to the "end all." GaiGai used this little glass bottle for every cut, scratch, sore, opening or wound, no matter the level of severity. I can honestly say that what came out of that cute container wasn't cute at all! The application felt like a lit match. That orangey substance was nothing more than coats of agony that up until a few years ago could still be seen on parts of my torso. What damage my body endured from that medicine was more difficult than me trying to breathe after all the running I did in the field at night.

Chapter 8

"Sicknesses"

My sister and I were born asthmatics. I felt bad for GaiGai. Along with duties of caring for our much older grandfather, who by now could only eat foods out of a blender that looked just like baby food, she had to figure out how to rid my sister and me from the unpredictable bouts we had with asthma.

Without warning, the wheezing would start. Before long, one, if not both, of us would find ourselves in a full-blown asthma attack. Back then, allergies had not been identified, and had we known it at the time, the feather pillows we slept on every night would have been destroyed. Later in life, we learned that we were highly allergic to feathers, and our down pillows had been the direct cause of so many of outbreaks.

During our years living with GaiGai, she diligently tried to find ways to rid us of this debilitating aliment. When a teaspoon of whiskey failed and our faces were too exhausted to lean out a window for fresh air, she would drive us around town for hours in hopes of us falling asleep.

Other times, weird ladies would stop by and pull our toes out of their sockets while we held Chihuahuas that were promised to, "inhale the asthma away." Nothing ever worked. Eventually, the asthma attacks would subside on their own but GaiGai thought it was proof that one of the two methods worked, and so she continued subjecting my sister and I to the ridiculous rituals.

One of the women, who came with her dog, smoked. My sister and I found this time extremely entertaining because GaiGai would stare her down like she was exhaling gold dust. Our grandmother saw tobacco as another form of medication. Any time someone that smoked came to our house, she couldn't wait to collect the end parts of their cigarettes when they left. In the kitchen drawer next to the sink, a very large amount of tobacco was collected, tightly wrapped in cellophane.

Any time we got stung by a wasp, hornet or anything with wings, GaiGai would grab the "ci-gau-rrett-ee" bag of tobacco. After spitting directly on the swollen bump, she would slap a clump of tobacco right on top where it remained until she decided that the "poison" had been drawn out.

Anyone outside of our family that happened to see a brown glob on our arm automatically knew what had happened. Nobody in their right mind would have partaken in such preposterousness, but GaiGai proudly did. Her belief system, I know, came with her when she moved here directly from Greece.

Metamucil was an interesting medicine. After our PauPou finished his breakfast every morning, he would reach for this rather large white container. My brother said that it was suppose to be taken with water or some kind of liquid. Whether it was because she didn't believe my brother or the fact that she couldn't read in English, GaiGai would instruct PauPou to swallow a spoon full of white powdery-crystals. My brother, sister, and I used to sit there with puckered faces and gag uncontrollably for him. I was so thankful this particular medicine was only for adults. PauPou tried to eat every meal with us.

If he was too sick and had been in bed more than three days, my sister and I would help GaiGai sponge bathe him. I wouldn't exactly call it a medicine, but our grandmother insisted on using a certain kind of soap on him at all times.

Lava soap was not a fun soap. Lava soap did not even smell nice. It was wrapped in a reddish package that to me, felt just like a piece of soft-grit sandpaper. GaiGai thought it would clean away the "diseases" from his body. When we finished, she would quickly point out how much better his completion looked. I felt sorry for him. Of course he had more color, skin has a way of reacting that way when blood is forced so close to the surface.

There is one sickness I struggle my whole life trying to forget about. GaiGai never went to the doctor. I don't recall her ever getting a cold, fever or even a headache. Aside from her china-cabinet medicine, I never once saw her pop a pill. There is no way to describe the bizarre, untreated illness GaiGai had.

On particularly trying days when it seemed my brother, sister, and I couldn't get along, our grandmother would become extremely exhausted. There really wasn't ever a clear indication that GaiGai was going to have one of her "episodes" because I promise, if any of us had known one of them was coming, we wouldn't ever be the one closet to her. For some ungodly reason, GaiGai would start shaking and complaining that she was weak. Grabbing the one of us nearest to her, she would throw our hand up under her dress and rake it across this oblong growth next to her vagina that felt just like a small child's head. I didn't know what it was. I didn't care. If I was the one stuck under her, I would fight like a caged animal to get as far away as I could from whatever was stationed under that woman's panties.

When there actually came a day that all of us were feeling well and getting along, GaiGai would dress the three of us up and take us into town to see some of her friends.

Chapter 9

"Luelle, Udelle, and all of GaiGai's friends"

GaiGai needed adult conversation. So with my brother, sister and me all piled into her car, we would drive to town across from the post office to see her friends, Luelle and Udelle. The house belonged to Luelle, and when her sister, Udelle from Florida, would come, GaiGai would be called so she could see them at the same time. We knew they were home when the rocking chairs on Luelle's front porch were placed in a seating position. Down South, people turn the chairs and prop them against their house backwards, when they are not. I enjoyed the location of her house. When we were allowed outside, I would sit on her steps and listen to passing trains race directly through town while the engineers blew their whistles on demand.

When we had the torturous duty of sitting inside with the sisters and GaiGai on Luelle's extremely uncomfortable couch, we would take turns making farting noises with the plastic that covered it. After a while, Luelle would ask my brother to get, "the candy jar."

This jar sat on an end table baking in the sun-filled window, all day, every day. After watching her struggle to open the Mason jar for some time, she would have to ask my brother to help her. Big deal, we didn't even like peppermint. We weren't allowed to refuse any. If we did, GaiGai would "fix us" the minute we got back home. I personally enjoyed watching

Luelle struggle as she attempted to break up the massive ball of goo with her fat little fingers. As far as I was concerned, she deserved to sweat. After all, I never saw her eat any of the candy she offered us.

GaiGai demanded that we were to be respectful at all times. She expected us to have superior manners, especially when we were around others. If one of us did anything that she felt was unacceptable, she would rapidly open and shut her mouth, while her bottom lip struggled to hold in her dentures.

The words "fix us" was not the broken English we wanted to hear. Any time she made eye contact and bit her lip only to whisper the words, "I'll fix you," we knew that the minute we got home we were going to get a beating, only forgotten by the many more received in the future. I got "fixed" a lot.

The first Monday of every month GaiGai drove to the beauty parlor. Most of the time, my brother was allowed to stay at home but on occasions, he had to come with us. The beauty parlor was in the house of a woman who had, over the years, become another one of my grandmother's friends.

Her name was Mildred, and her house was fascinating. Her yard and flower gardens looked like pictures from a Southern Living magazine. There was no surprise that my siblings and I wanted to spend our time there outside. Smelling the lavish greenery while folding up fern leaves with bugs trapped inside were among the things we could do there. She had these very unique gourds that were made especially for birds. I loved lying on the ground and watching them go in and out their houses, chirping and tweeting. I always wanted to look inside of them and see the little babies that might be sleeping, but they were so high up in the trees. Roaming her grounds was amazing. But there was another reason we liked going to Mildred's, a private, sinister one that we never said out loud.

Mrs. Mildred had an older sister who, at birth, was born slightly retarded and partially paralyzed on the left side of her body. If we were lucky, while looking through the right window at the right time, we could catch a glimpse of her, shuffling slowly from room to room talking "gibberish" to herself. While Mildred worked on her clients in the parlor, my brother, sister and I would take turns, discretely watching her sister. We knew we shouldn't and as afraid as we were of getting "fixed," for some strange reason, we couldn't help ourselves. Personally, I thought GaiGai was worse.

When her hair was almost finished, we would go in and wait on the floor next to her. Periodically, Mrs. Mildred's sister would creep in. GaiGai had the audacity to ask her all these unnecessary, mind-blowing questions knowing that Mildred's sister could not talk. Oh, and it didn't stop with just one or two questions; GaiGai went on and on until Mildred would finally intervene and stop the craziness all together.

I don't know how Mildred did it, but she managed to send GaiGai home with the same blue-colored hair she had when she came. I guess Mrs. Mildred had the "natural rinse" in her parlor too.

When GaiGai wasn't spending time with Luelle, Udelle, or Mildred, she made us go with her to Mary Murray's house.

For the longest time, we called her Mary Myrdal until we realized that GaiGai had been mispronouncing it based on her lack of understanding the English language. Mary Murray was, by far, the scariest woman I had ever seen. Standing almost six feet and weighing no more than one hundred pounds, the only proof we had that she was still alive was her ability to walk.

Her face was gaunt and as white as a ghost. She must have used a half bottle of foundation on her face every day but the makeup was clearly too dark for her complexion. She wore deep red lipstick that made her teeth look even more yellow and dirty than they already were. Her hair looked like a flyaway scouring pad that was ready to disintegrate from all the cleaning of pots and pans. Her fingernails were so long that my brother, sister and I kept a five-foot circumference just to insure our own safety.

Her house fit her appearance perfectly. She lived in this enormously decrepit Victorian that had probably been painted just after it was initially built. The shutters, with the exception of one, had all fallen off. Hers was the only house we had never been invited into. I was glad. I thought that at any moment, her house would collapse. Dying in her house with her was not the way I wanted to go.

GaiGai treated all of her friends the same. She gossiped negatively about every one of them. Our entire drive home, no matter with which friend we had spent our afternoon, said friend suddenly became a person we had never met or known before. GaiGai's attitude towards her friends in front of her friends was clearly not the same one she presented to us. All the terrible things she would say just to get us all dressed up and back to see them a few weeks later.

Chapter 10

"Friends of our own"

After living with GaiGai and PauPou for some time, we learned that just a few miles down the road, three separate families with children close to our ages also lived. Whenever we complained of loneliness or desired the kinship of other children other than each other, GaiGai would drive us farther down the dirt road to a quaint little house, passing only two others.

There, a brother and sister lived with their parents. The boy was my brother's age and the girl, exactly the same age as my sister and I. My brother, sister, and I loved going to their house. They had all these wonderful board games and toys that we thought were only used as store window decorations, not items you could actually buy.

The girl had the most beautiful dolls I had ever seen. She had so many Barbies that we got to play with three or more at the same time. She was so lucky and spoiled. She didn't take care of her toys. I couldn't believe what she did with her dolls, especially. With a pair of scissors, she cut most of her doll's hair almost completely off. Then she would add makeup to their faces with magic markers and pink nail polish.

Her brother was just as ungrateful. He had filled bookshelves. Most of them were thrown about his bedroom floor while the rest of them were still in their original wrapping, never opened. Since my brother was an avid reader, I can only imagine what he was thinking every time he sat in the boy's room, salivating at all the brightly colored book covers, and imagining what they could possibly be about.

As impressed as we were with their toys, the clothes in their closets, was overwhelming. Hangers and hangers of every color of store-bought outfits you could think of imploded within, some with tags still attached. I never saw a single hand-sewn one. At first, it seemed almost unnatural. So for a while I avoided going near them altogether, no matter how curious I was about what was on the top shelf.

When they got tired of watching us play with their incredible selection of stuff, we would all go outside and take turns riding their go-cart that Santa had given them the previous Christmas. Their dad had designed and made a real cool dirt track with bumps we could jump while driving.

My brother, sister and I never had as much fun as we did when we took our turns behind the wheel of that incredible moving piece of metal. With four giant tires throwing out clouds of dust and no instructions on how it operated, it's amazing that none of us broke a bone. When the gas tank was empty and our stomachs were in so much pain from all the laughter, we jumped on their trampoline and defy death in a whole new way.

On rainy days when none of us could go out, we would sit in front of their television set. My brother, sister and I loved TV. The one that GaiGai and PauPou had broke and now served as a random piece of furniture in their living room. The chance of watching one was not one we were willing to pass up.

The only way the brother and sister ever had a chance of luring the three of us away from the TV was by listening to music from the radios each of them had in their own rooms. I'm not sure what my brother and his friend did, but my sister and I lay for hours with our friend, staring at the tiny holes in the brown rectangle convinced that the musical group, The Bee Gees, were singing directly to us.

Every once and a while my sister and I played with another pair of sisters who lived in one of the houses we passed to get to the brother's and sister's with all the fun things.

Although these sisters were two years apart in age, they looked so much alike we often called them by each other's names. We liked them just as much as the brother and sister. Sometimes all seven of us played together.

The only time we all didn't get along was when this really, really fat girl who lived in the very first house down our dirt road waddled up to play. During the early to mid 1970's, we rarely came across a large person, particularly a giant one, so when the fat girl came to play, it was hard not to take notice.

Whenever she talked, I had a really hard time understanding her. Initially, I thought she had a speech problem but that idea was quickly dismissed. When three separate chins are all fighting at the same time to be heard, nothing makes sense.

Her entire body was rolls and rolls of fat separated only by deepened lines. Her thighs were especially interesting because they looked like one fused mass of flesh, with two feet pointing outwards at the end. Watching her sit was exhausting. Raw, irritated skin between her legs periodically released crumbled talcum powder her mother put there to relieve the burning. Her eyes, although a pretty brown, were so sunken in on account of her overly round face and, as far as I could tell, they looked only partially opened. Her hair never had a chance to dry. All the sweating, along with her mother's decision to keep her hair short, made her neck look like a big overcooked sausage.

Trying to incorporate her in our play that didn't take into account the obvious was impossible. Every stinkin' time she tripped over her own fatness and bounced off the trampoline, she would stomp off crying like a little butthole. During every episode once the crying stopped, she would start blurting out some kind of baloney about losing her baby weight by the end of summer and that once she had, we would never be able to "talk about her when she wasn't around!" That was never going to happen.

God had a way of punishing me for my lack of sensitivity towards the fat girl. One Friday night when PauPou had gotten really sick, of all the houses I could have stayed, GaiGai made me be the one forced to sleep over the fat girl's house. There were so many times that my sister and I both had a sleepover at the other houses but for some reason, GaiGai decided to separate us, proving once again how much she detested me.

While I imagined my brother and sister enjoying their time away from our mundane routine, I was forced to play with the big girl. I had never seen her parents before but as much as I shouldn't have been surprised, I was shocked! Her parents were much larger than she. I didn't know the human body had the ability to stretch out that far but I learned a lot about them the weekend I stayed.

Their house was extremely smelly. I think the couch used to be a light green but since they let their dogs sleep all over it, I couldn't be sure. The amount of dog hair that blew all over the house from leaving the front and back door wide open was just plain gross. But making me watch their dogs "sit and be pretty" so they could be rewarded an actual raw pork chop as if I would be positively blown away by the whole dog trick experience scared the absolute crap out of me.

When supper time came, I was introduced to this strange aluminum plate, separated by three indentions called a TV dinner. I was baffled how food could be served or eaten this way. From what I observed, they ate like this all the time. Instead of sitting at a table, they preferred eating directly in front of their television, wedged in huge chairs that I don't think should have been able to lean back within inches of the floor but somehow they managed. I didn't dare eat mine. I didn't know how. I was afraid I would get sick, especially when their breathing increased with every bite, so when the big girl finished her third and reached over to finish mine, I declared her the "clean plate club winner" and excused myself straight to her room.

As soon as they were finished eating, I immediately asked to go to bed. The fat girl left me to change into my night clothes and while she ate her dessert, I lay in this old iron bed that squeaked a great deal. Lookling around her room, I noticed a poster of Shawn Cassidy starring at me. I became so angry for having been trapped here in a slumber party from hell that a bubble swelled in my throat. Pretending like I was looking back at GaGai, I proceeded to cuss and "fix her" in ways no young girl should ever think about, in ways I didn't want her to ever forget.

I barely survived my stay. A week later, we started school.

Chapter 11

"Good Ole School Days"

I absolutely hated going to school. Getting out of bed during the cold winter was dreadful. I had always been an insomniac. I attributed it to my father's indiscretions with me at night so falling asleep was not a regular occurrence. Getting dressed in a room that averaged about thirty degrees was not something I looked forward to, either. Not even the smell of GaiGai's cooking could make facing another day of relentless name calling and finger pointing tolerable.

I had determined that the closer people lived to town, the wealthier they were. Houses directly in town were grand. Their lawns were perfectly manicured. They had colorful flowers nicely designed in shapes and groupings. From the bus window, I swore I could smell roses.

Those of us that lived farther from town rode the school bus a long while. Sitting in my seat, watching my life pass at every stop, gave me lots of time to self-reflect. I thought about things children my age wouldn't seem feasible. I wondered what it would be like if I was one of the "lucky" children whose mother stood outside, waving to them and the bus driver as they boarded. I pictured myself in their houses, in my own room with ruffled curtains that matched my bedspread. On my walls would hang ballerina pictures because I would be taking ballet lessons in tutus like the girls I saw carrying in specially embroidered bags. I

spent almost every day going back and forth to school,
wishing I was someone else.

I was someone else. I was the girl everyone
heard coming down the hallway from the sound my
corduroy pants made as the bell bottoms rubbed each
other in unison. The one wearing a dress I outgrew and
which now buttoned as a blouse. I was the quiet one
with the braided hair looped up like giant earrings on
both sides of my head because GaiGai was still stuck in
the 1930's. The one I felt everyone stared at and when
they said their prayers before bed, thanking God he
didn't make them, me.

The teacher I had seemed nice but when she was
around the other ones, she pointed at me as she covered
her mouth, which made me rather uncomfortable. At
my old school, I overheard my first grade teacher tell
my father how smart I was, but this school made me
insecure. I never held my hand up or participated in
class even though I knew all the answers.

My sister handled the transition just fine. The
two of us had always been placed in separate classes
since no one could tell us apart, so I couldn't wait until
recess where I would at least be around someone
familiar. My sister was a social butterfly. She loved
school. She couldn't wait to go. She made friends
easily. Everything she was, I was not.

On occasion when a swing was free, I would go
as high as I could and pretend I was in the backyard of
my make-believe fancy house with my make- believe
fancy family. If another child dared yell up at me that I
had swung long enough and it was now their turn, I

would ignore them and swing even higher. Fancy people didn't have to share. Fancy people didn't have to give up what they had to someone else. Fancy people were waited *on*, not waiting *for*. As long as I was swinging, I was fancy too.

I didn't see my brother at school. He was two grades ahead of my sister and me, so I never had a chance to be around him until the day was over and I would see him on the bus. The ride was so long. As a matter of fact, we were one of the last ones to get off aside of our playmates: the fat girl, the sisters and the brother and sister.

For some strange reason, on our way home, this one black boy use to tie my brother to the seat he sat in every single day with a rope. I have no idea why. My brother was so involved with his book reading that he never noticed. I of course, would get so angry because I was afraid my brother would get stuck and left there. I never understood why my brother let this boy treat him this way. But every day, I witnessed the weird ritual and every day, the bus driver would shake his head at my brother untangling himself as I stood mystified by the stupidity of it all.

Just once, I wished my brother would have pulled his head out of his book long enough to punch that black boy in the face. He never did, and after a while I just accepted that my brother was used to being mistreated. His way of reacting to things, was accepting them. Nothing and no one could change that part of him; sadly, not even the mean black boy could.

Walking down the driveway was such a relief. I couldn't wait to see GaiGai and PauPou. I didn't care that there was probably lots of work to do or new handmade corduroys to try on. I was happy that the school day was over and the only thing that mattered now, was what we would be eating for dinner.

Chapter 12

"Poorer Than Poor"

We had run out of milk. A few miles down the road was a little convenient store. GaiGai driving us there in the dark without wrecking the car seemed more like a survival drill than a trip to the store. The only time she drove at night was if there was an emergency. Not having milk to drink constituted just that.

When we got there, I of course had to be the one to run fast "inni and a outti" as GaiGai would say it. Holding tight the ninety-eight cents to get in and out is exactly what I had in mind.

Apparently, within the week, the price of milk had gone from ninety-eight to ninety- nine cents. I didn't know what to do. I was afraid of leaving the store without the milk GaiGai insisted we needed but I had no way of producing the extra penny either. I stood for the longest time looking at the clerk as she counted out the money. She could tell I was very nervously embarrassed. She knew who I was. Everyone in town knew who the "little Greek girls" were. Back then, there was no such thing as "give a penny, take a penny."

After counting out the money for the second time, she and I both knew what had to be done. I took the milk. Not outside into the car but down the aisle to the glass doors. I put back what couldn't be bought with a coin most people now let stay on the ground.

I never looked at a penny the same way after that. Every time I see a round piece of copper, I immediately think of a gallon of milk. That's what a penny means to me -- a whole gallon of white wishing and wanting and a sweet taste of nothing, if you don't have enough money to get it.

We returned home that night empty handed. GaiGai took water and spoonfuls of powdered creamer she used in her coffee and mixed them together. We drank that "milk," the poor-persons' version of it anyway. We didn't dare say a word about the taste. Instead, we talked about Christmas and the fact that it was only a month away.

Hearing that lights on a tree could catch on fire, GaiGai drug out a beat-up box from the hall closet and told us that her silver one was better. My brother, sister and I did not agree. Every single branch was encased by a brown papered tube that took the three of us all day to individually remove without damaging their feather-like endings.

Each branch had painted so that it could easily be matched with its proper location. Throughout the years, those tips were no longer visible, making placing each branch in the correct hole much harder. When the tree was finally put together, none of us felt much like decorating. Besides, there was only a handful of decorations to put on the tree anyway. On the curtains in the dining room where the tree stood, GaiGai attached two stained stockings that belonged to my father and aunt when they lived there as children. My father's now belonged to my brother, and my aunt's, my sister and me. A modest poinsettia centered the table. Once it was placed there, the doors were shut and stayed that way until Christmas.

Exactly one week before Christmas, GaiGai insisted my sister and I accompany her as she delivered hand-crocheted bedroom shoes to all of her friends. This was by far the most degrading expression of giving I in which I would ever be made to participate. Ringing the doorbell and personally handing GaiGai's friends a present wrapped in previously used paper was humiliating. Knowing they were in monogrammed boxes from the most expensive store in town we retrieved from the dumpster on Saturdays before dusk was laconically insulting. We did it anyway. My sister and I didn't have a choice.

Every time I thought about Christmas and what I might get, I prayed to God I wouldn't get one of the boxes we stole with a pair of bedroom shoes GaiGai made in it for me.

Like every child, the three of us counted down the days until Santa Claus would come. The idea of him bringing me a Barbie on account of my good behavior was overwhelming.

Christmas Eve finally came. I decided to stay up long enough to see this man in red for myself. I heard a noise. The sound was coming directly from the dining room down the hall. I could not believe it! I couldn't stop smiling. I quietly and gently tiptoed until I came to the door where I was convinced I would see Santa placing all our wonderful toys. With my hand sweating with anticipation, I turned the knob to see a large figure putting candy in one of the stockings. Trembling there with my mouth wide open, the shadowy figure turned around and looked right at me.

There was no such thing as Santa. Not unless he was actually a she with blue-tinted hair, fist waving at me to go back to bed. The only candy put in those stockings was from the bag of melted orange jellies my grandfather kept next to his bed. The gifts we would open would be only one each, new corduroy outfits with an added seam line that could easily be taken out every time we hit a growth spurt.

Only GaiGai will know why she never told us that there was no such thing as man named Santa Claus who wore a red suit and landed on houses in a sleigh with eight reindeer but, I sure wished she would have told us all along. Only one thing got me through my disappointment . . . Christmas food.

Chapter 13

"The Foods"

The foods on Christmas day were by far the best of the entire year. Most was prepared weeks in advance while we were in school. In the evenings, we liked to help because GaiGai always left us batter in the mixing bowls before we had to clean them.

On the day of Christmas dinner, there was nothing like the smell of lamb cooking with potatoes, drowning in lemony white wine sauce with fresh oregano with basil. All morning long and throughout the day, we did everything we could to take our minds off that hypnotic smell. When dinner time came, we couldn't stop!

Homemade orzo (pasta), spanakopeta (spinich pie), dolmades, (rice-wrapped grape leaves), mousaka, (eggplant dish) and pastichio (baked macaroni) were laid all over the dining room table. There were no manners behind the madness. The tastes turned us into people we didn't recognize. Eating food while it was popping hot and burning the roof of my mouth didn't stop me from grabbing more and more . . . until my stomach felt like it was going to explode.

Desserts were even better. Eating as much kolourakia and kourabiedes cookies as we could before GaiGai cut the baklava (walnut Danish) was a challenge my brother, sister, and I were all willing to take. Eating Loukoumathes (fried doughnuts with honey) while drinking warm buttermilk was good too.

Nothing compared to the Christmas feast. The only thing that maybe came close was, New Year's.

To celebrate the New Year, GaiGai made a very special kind of bread. Vasilopita was named after Saint Basil. The dough had to be baked round because its circular shape represented a family that never ends. My brother, sister, and I would hover over GaiGai when the time came for her to cut the special bread. The first cut piece was always reserved and dedicated to God. The second slice was for Jesus and thirdly, Saint Basil. Thereafter, the head of every household starting with the father came next, the mother and on to the first eldest child. Vasilopita bread was the sole purpose of celebrating the New Year. Whoever got the piece holding the coin baked inside, (a silver dollar or fifty-cent piece) also got good fortune the entire year. I used to eat one piece after another in hopes of getting the one with the coin. All children did.

How was I to know that by eating the last of the desserts and the final piece of vasilopita without getting the "good luck token," everything I had become accustomed to living with GaiGai and PauPou, would suddenly change.

Chapter 14

"From Five to Four"

PauPou was getting sicker. He was no longer able to keep foods down no matter how many different methods GaiGai tried. He struggled to rest in the hospital bed brought into our house for him. Afraid that he might fall out or something worse, GaiGai reluctantly placed him in a nursing home on the other side of town.

Every single day, we spent as much time as we could with our PauPou. None of us wanted him to think he had been abandoned. GaiGai never seemed pleased with the way the nurses bathed him, so going later in the day allowed her the peace of at least thinking that a group effort made by the four of us doing same thing was better.

The smell in the nursing home was a kind that no matter how hard you tried, you couldn't ignore. After a while we all started to smell like the poor old people, half asleep, collecting dust as they lingered in their wheelchairs along both sides of the walls in the hallways. Coming or going, timing was irrelevant. The odor of invisible urine, flowed from room to room, no matter how many times the janitor mobbed the floors.

I had a hard time emotionally going daily to see my grandfather. Any time I overheard an elderly person refer to this place as their residence, that person would not wake up the following day. I didn't want my PauPou to go to sleep and die here. I didn't want my

PauPou to die at all. I was so frustrated not knowing what would happen and more scared of what might. I didn't find any comfort in being told that our aunt who lived in the north was on her way to help us.

Until then, we continued our visits with PauPou. The one thing he seemed to enjoy was the brief period of time we spent playing his favorite card games with the pennies GaiGai kept folded up in an envelope on the inside pouch of her pocket book. He always won. The only difference now is that we let him, every single time.

As he tired, GaiGai ended our game playing. Speaking only in Greek, she liked to lean over him to say her goodbyes. I took great notice in how they interacted. I couldn't get over a man that once stood 6'2" and weighed close to 250 pounds now had trouble holding up his own neck. I never imagined that a man I had only seen in great positions would all of a sudden become baby-like in a fetal one.

Watching my grandmother rub my grandfather's forehead was a direct reflection of pure love. I wondered what they were thinking when they looked at each other and if they imagined who would suffer more. My GaiGai having to go on living without her beloved, and perhaps he would have to die all alone, without his. The ordeal was as beautiful as it was heart-wrenching. Life without the both of them in it was too hard for me to think about but as hard as I tried not to, that's all I did.

My negative thoughts consumed me. My anxiety tortured me. The phone call we got the week following my aunt's arrival destroyed every part of my being. Everything good was bad. Everything now became then and everything I knew forced my spirit directly into a permanent prison of ultimate uncertainty and uncontrollable grief.

I never cried as hard as I did the day we buried my grandfather. People from all over the states of Georgia and Alabama came to say goodbye to the "finest man that ever lived." For hours, the cars came and went. I was unaware of the magnitude of people that knew the man I called PauPou. I had never been told of the hardships other families had faced and had sought refuge in my grandparents' house, or about the number of men my grandfather hired even though he didn't need them just so they could provide for their families. I was completely shocked when I heard about all the people at the funeral who had eaten for free on several occasions in my grandparents' restaurant because they couldn't afford to pay. The reality of who my grandfather actually was became positively overwhelming, and everything around me seemed to move in slow motion.

The gun shots were loud. GaiGai didn't do a very good job receiving the presented flag. I kept hearing her say something about how much PauPou loved, "the blue, the red, and the white colors." I distinctly recall my grandparents loving this country so much that they changed their last name to become more Americanized. When people from town made comments about my sister and I being Greek girls, GaiGai would quickly interject, telling them she was "American" and that my sister and I were "American" girls too.

Leaning over and pressing my head against my grandfather's heart while he lay in his casket, his pacemaker ticked no more. Looking directly at his closed eyes, I knew he would be sleeping forever. Turning and facing so much black collectively gathering crumbled my ten-year-old heart into so many pieces that part of me wished, I had died too. I don't remember much after that.

I wasn't ready for his death. I wasn't ready for my life to change. I wasn't ready for the news that in the days following, GaiGai would have to go to Greece. I just simply wasn't ready. Her leaving meant only one thing. My brother, sister and I would have to live with our father all over again. We would have to be in a new town, attending a new school, in a new house with a very new mother that we had only met briefly two times before.

Chapter 15

"The Final Goodbye"

GaiGai left. We watched her. No words will ever come close to describing how a broken heart feels. Nobody will ever convince me that there is a harsher pain in the world. Standing there holding back my tears as she pulled the door against her legs, I thought I would collapse. Accepting that my grandmother would not be in my life, as a part of my life, when she had been in all of it was going to be as foreign as the country she was heading to.

I would miss her. I would miss everything about her. I would miss the way she smelled. I would miss the way her arms felt when I wrapped myself around them with my own. I would miss how she confused words with made-up ones, while her blue hair straightened in frustration. I would miss the way she cooked and how it made our house smell. I would miss her abilities to take nothing and turn it into something so amazingly beautiful. I would even miss the way she called my name when I was about to get "fixed" for doing things I shouldn't have done.

I knew that GaiGai would probably not miss me. I knew that she would never love me the way she loved my brother and sister. Everything I ever wanted from her, I would have to give myself. Still, I couldn't handle the awkwardness of the moment. When she stuck her hand out the window and waved, I didn't dare say goodbye.

The red dirt had not even settled and my father was already starting. Packing our belongings into the trunk of the car, our new mother sat in the front without saying a single word. Her eeriness was just the prelude to all the terrible things waiting for us just a few hours down the road.

Chapter 16

"Three Years Too Many"

My father made it perfectly clear that he didn't want us in his life. He told us on the day we moved in, that we would only be guests. In his house, guests had to pay for their rent.

The only thing different about my father was that ever since he had gotten a girlfriend that was now my stepmother, the sexual abuse abruptly came to a halt. I looked forward to memories being made in a house that didn't involve my father and me in the same bed. Her taking my place was the best thing that happened during the three years we were forced to live there.

My stepmother didn't look anything like my real mother. She didn't look like a mother at all. If I would have ever seen her on a playground and didn't know she was in her early twenties, I would have asked her to play with me. She had jet-black hair and yellow-colored skin with a petite nose that was virtually flat. My sister and I were taller than she, and there was no way we would ever fit into her size 4 shoes. She was a tiny Filipino who came from the Philippines that could also speak the language. She looked just like a little girl. She was absolutely perfect for my father.

We seldom saw her. She worked two full-time jobs. My father told us that they met at the hospital where he worked in the lab, and she was his boss. Wearing a white coat was the closest my father was ever going to get to being a nice Greek doctor. His work had shift variations, but most of the time, he worked from three in the afternoon till eleven in the evening.

While we were in school, my father spent his time conjuring ways to torture us. I have no doubt in my mind that my father specifically picked a house many miles away from the private Catholic school to which we had to walk back and forth on purpose. He knew we would hate having to walk so far in the heat.

Opening the kitchen door, there was no GaiGai there to greet us. There were no sounds of pots and pans clanging together or smells atop the stove cooking -- unless you count the one coming from the black sharpie my father left with a note, cussing us out because he saw finger streaks next to the burners.

He prided himself in leaving us instructions. He did so daily. On perfectly cut partially used typing paper he got from work, black-sharpie-written ridiculousness would be scattered all over "his " house for us to read. Instead of doing homework or playing with friends like normal children, the three of us spent hours perfecting everything he determined less than perfect so he could judge our efforts when he returned home from work.

Climbing the stairs to our rooms only to see more paper was almost amusing. There were so many rules to follow when it came to the bedrooms. Order was first and foremost. Empty coat hangers had to hang at the very left of our closets. Iron-pressed, long-sleeved shirts (previously inspected) had to be placed second, and finally dress pants. Shorts and short-sleeved shirts had to line our drawers by color and be folded exactly the way he taught us. Every night before we went to bed, the three of us had to leave our polished shoes right outside our doors.

There was nothing quite like the surprise of shoes beating up my face in the middle of the night because of a failed inspection. I never got used to that, and he never got tired of busting my lips with the heels and soles while my sister balled up next to me, pretending she was asleep.

His written rules were insane. His verbal ones were however, repulsive. Since "his children" were perfect, the words, "I thought" and "I forgot" did not exist. If any one of us got caught saying one of the "unspeakables," the violator would have to pay my father five dollars. If any article of clothing was determined to be unacceptable, he expected five dollars. Not fast enough, five dollars. Not clean enough, five dollars. Improper order, five dollars.

The entire relationship we had with our father centered around five-dollar bills. Having five dollars readily available and making five dollars to give my father were the only concerns my father had for our existence.

Every afternoon my stepmother came home to grab a quick nap before her next shift. On Fridays, she gave each of us five dollars in quarters for the following week's school lunches. The fifteen dollars the three of us were given was the quickest money my father ever made for doing absolutely nothing. My stepmother never knew my father took our money. My father knew we would never tell her.

In order to pay my father, my sister and I cleaned people's houses. To sustain my father's demand of his five-dollar rule, I typically cleaned houses four to five times a week while my brother cut grass. I don't know exactly how long it took, but it seemed like forever before he had made enough money to buy his own gas can and lawn mower. Until then, my sister and I picked up additional cleanings to ensure my brother would always have a five-dollar bill on hand.

My God, there were so many times I just wanted to take a five-dollar bill and shove it down my father's throat. I wanted to slowly suffocate him so he would not be able to ever ask for another one, ever again. I knew better. He had too many pretty-paper squares with black sharpies to let even muteness get in the way of his precious money collecting.

Our life there in that house is something I still struggle daily to forget.

Three very long years passed, but those three years seemed more like a lifetime. The summer of that year, my brother hit puberty. He started to sweat a lot and my father enjoyed making fun of him. He especially enjoyed mastering his skills of verbal defecation directly in my brother's face. Once, he went too far. Out of absolute fear, my brother's nose exploded and blood shot out everywhere. What my father did to my brother as a result of his misfortune, is a memory that has haunted me my entire life.

Instead of trying to stop the bleeding, my father made my brother keep his face down so blood would continue flowing. In an attempt to help my brother, against my father's will, my sister and I grabbed table napkins. We vigorously tried to cover my brother's face while my father continued beating him uncontrollably. The minutes of madness continued on and on but my father just wouldn't quit.

He ordered me to get a pot kept underneath the kitchen sink. I didn't want to do that, but I had no choice. Almost as much blood as when my mother had slit her wrists weighed down the red linens heavily. Droplets that had gotten on the walls and floor had to wiped immediately and tossed with the others into the pot my father had taken from me. Running water briefly over the soggy mess, I had no idea what lesson my father was about to teach.

We were not allowed to close our eyes. My father took my sister's face and mine, slammed them together and demanded us to watch my brother drink the entire bloody contents. Every time he gagged, or worse vomited back into the pot, he had to start all over again. We spent hours watching my father almost drown my brother into the pot until out of nowhere, he became bored and decided to get ready for work.

My father's violence and hatred escalated without warning. My sister and I were very afraid that my father might possible kill our brother if given another opportunity like his nosebleed. Almost a month later, my father started picking on my brother and his changing body.

My father didn't think my brother was doing a good enough job bathing, but it was actually due to a lack of underarm deodorant. My brother didn't really know how to buy nor did he have enough money at the time for the spray. My sister and I had fallen behind as well and didn't have any extra to give him. The electric and water bills for the previous month were higher than usual, and the three of us barely had enough to cover all the amounts due.

We would have had our "reserve" money our father insisted we keep in a little savings account at the bank he used without our permission. He drained all three of our accounts for a fish aquarium he always wanted but said we did instead. None of us could allow ourselves a mistake. None of us had a five-dollar bill to spare. Not this time.

Chapter 17

"Her Birthday Gift"

My brother had just left for his scheduled lawn cuttings. My father was so upset he had missed him. Returning home from the hardware store, my father was hoping for a chance at bathing my brother with the wire metal scrub brush he had purchased just for him.

I couldn't believe how much worse my father was getting. I didn't know how I was going to find my brother and prevent my father from fulfilling his demonic desires but I knew that if I didn't, my brother would surely die. I couldn't let that happen.

As soon as my father backed down the driveway for an appointment he made for his car, I ran throughout the entire neighborhood and beyond, searching for my brother. I don't exactly remember how long it took, but I was so happy when I heard the sound of a lawnmower and even happier when I saw it was my brother's. He could tell immediately that something was very wrong.

When I told him of our father's plan, we both agreed that my brother could never return. We didn't know where he should go, we just knew that anywhere else would be better.

At about almost dinner time, my sister had finished her house cleanings and the two of us waited, praying our brother would find some place safe to go. Periodically, the two of us walked up and down our driveway, making sure we didn't see him coming back.

On about the third trip, we saw a car driving slowly at us, and before we had a chance to react, my brother yelled out our names from the passenger window.

Parking the car and getting out, the lady with my brother told us it was her birthday and the three of us were her special gift. She was a social worker. She wanted us to pack suitcases with as many clothes as we could and wait until the police came. She explained that this was a common practice since in most cases, fighting typically broke out whenever children were being taken away. She wanted a chance to explain to my father his legal rights, and although I knew what she was trying to say, I didn't care. I just wanted her to take us out of there.

Time was on our side. The building where such family matters took place was closing soon. She needed to find a "foster family" for us to stay the night until the following morning, where we would all be joining in family court of law.

On the way to the Department Of Pensions and Security (the proper name at that time), our social worker asked us to "keep a lookout" for our father so that if we happened to pass him, she could turn and go back to explain the situation.

Not even to the end of our neighborhood, there came his car. Not a single one of us said a word. I almost found it humorous that none of us even turned our heads. All three of us just stared in unison directly at the back of the social worker's long front seat.

The very next morning, my father and stepmother lost all their parental rights. My brother, sister, and I became, "wards of the court." Simply stated, our parents were now the entire state of Alabama. Walking outside, I opened my arms as far as I could and hugged my brand new 97-degree mother and father. Their hug was the best hug I had ever received.

A week later, we moved into the Alabama Baptist Children's Home.

Chapter 18

"Fat and Tanned"

GaiGai came back from Greece. Everything was different now. My aunt from the north was the person my brother contacted, and with the help from the nuns at our school, she helped us escape my father's house that terrifying day. We were surprised that they had been keeping personal written documentation of their own against my father which made our removal eminent.

After a brief period of living with our aunt to rekindle our relationship with GaiGai, the transition proved too painful and the three of us returned back to the orphanage.

Overweight and very tanned, GaiGai went to the place where four years earlier we had all said our goodbyes. She went home. My brother, sister, and I went to visit her often, all the way through high school and college. We spent many holidays with her and introduced her to many of our adult friends.

On Thanksgiving Day, one month after my husband and I married, GaiGai passed away. She left her house to my brother, sister and me.

Epilogue

My brother is a veterinarian. He has been a very nice Greek doctor for over 22 years. He has never married.

My sister graduated college and is currently working on her master's degree. After many marital hardships, she ended her marriage after 21 years. She has a beautiful daughter and son. She has a new love in her life, one that calls her GaiGai now.

I graduated from college too, a whole year ahead because I was in love. For the very brief time we lived with my aunt up north, I made a little friend. We stayed pen pals. The day I graduated college, I had nowhere to go. My brother was still in medical school and my sister was married, continuing her own education. I did not have a plan.

My little friend did. He came. He drove 13 hours in a truck and after watching me graduate, then took me to the north where I have been ever since. We have been married more than 21 years. I have a wonderful life. I have an amazing son who is seventeen. Marrying my husband was the best decision I ever made, having my son was my second. All three of us work together in our family-owned business.

About The Author

Anna Löwenadler is a 1990 graduate of Troy State University (now Troy University) in Troy, Alabama. Her work of short stories has been published in the *Pittsburgh Post-Gazette.*

Author's Husband and Son

Elementary school attended by Author

CPSIA information can be obtained at www.ICGtesting.com
Printed in the USA
BVOW03s0555260314

348814BV00002B/234/P